You and Your Pet
Guinea Pig

Jean Coppendale

QED Publishing

First published in the UK in 2004 by
QED Publishing
A division of Quarto Publishing plc
The Fitzpatrick Building
188–194 York Way, London N7 9QP

A Catalogue record for this book is available from the British Library.

ISBN 1 84538 052 5

Written by Jean Coppendale
Consultant: Michaela Miller
Designed by Susi Martin
Editor: Gill Munton
All photographs by Jane Burton except
fruit on pages 20 and 21 by Chris Taylor
With many thanks to Melissa and Roy Payne
Picture of Squeaker on page 29 by Georgie Meek

Creative Director: Louise Morley
Editorial Manager: Jean Coppendale

Printed and bound in China

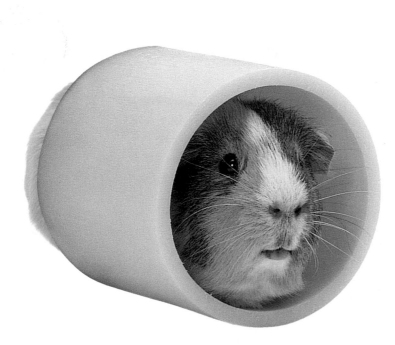

Words in **bold** are explained on page 32.

29,

18

6

1

13

14

'17 MAY 2014

30 MAY 2015

Contents

Your first guinea pig   4
Lots of guinea pigs   6
Which guinea pig?   8
Guinea pig shopping list   10
Getting ready   12
Saying hello   14
Handle with care   16
Looking after your guinea pig   18
Feeding your guinea pigs   20
Keep it clean   22
Your guinea pig's life cycle   24
Let's explore!   26
Saying goodbye   28
Guinea pig checklist   30
Parent's checklist   31
Guinea pig words   32
Index   32

Your first guinea pig

Guinea pigs can make lovely pets. Once they get to know you, they like to be stroked and held gently. But guinea pigs are not toys. They are small and fragile, and easily hurt. They also need a lot of looking after, because they must be kept clean and well fed.

▲ **Guinea pigs like to play outside.**

▶ **Guinea pigs can live for up to seven years.**

▼ The proper name for a guinea pig is a cavy.

Guinea pigs are fun and like to explore

▶ They may look shy, but guinea pigs like to run and play.

Lots of guinea pigs

Guinea pigs are all the same shape but have different markings and colourings.

◀ **Some guinea pigs, such as this red Agouti, are all one colour.**

▼ **These Alpaca guinea pigs have long, silky coats.**

▶This guinea pig has a big white stripe.

◀This grey and white guinea pig has rosetted fur.

▼This crested Sheltie guinea pig has long hair.

Which guinea pig?

Guinea pigs like to live in groups, so you should buy at least two. Buy two boys or two girls from the same **litter**.

Guinea pigs have long and short hair. A long-haired guinea pig will need to be brushed every day but all guinea pigs will enjoy being brushed.

Guinea pigs usually get on with rabbits, so you can keep a rabbit with your guinea pig to stop it getting lonely. But the two pets should be brought up together. Always keep an eye on them to make sure the rabbit does not bully the guinea pig.

▲ **A guinea pig and a rabbit can be good friends.**

▶ **Short-haired guinea pigs are easier to look after.**

Guinea pig shopping list

Your guinea pig will need

▶ **An indoor hutch**

▼ **An outdoor run**

◀ **Wood shavings**

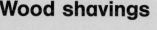

◀ **Hay for the bedding**

▶ **Two water bottles, one for the hutch and one for the run, and a bottle brush**

▶ **A scoop for cleaning out the hutch**

◀ **A carrier for trips to the vet**

◀ A gnawing block is needed to help teeth and gums stay healthy

▶ Two heavy food bowls, one for the hutch and one for the run

▲ Guinea pig food

Getting ready

Place the hutch in a warm, quiet spot if it is indoors. The hutch should have a closed-off area so that the guinea pig has a private place to sleep. The main part of the hutch should have an open, wire mesh front, so that the guinea pig can look out.

Put a layer of old newspaper on the floor of the hutch. Spread lots of wood shavings (or cat litter) on top of the newspaper. Put a layer of hay on top of this. Make sure there is lots of hay in the sleeping area for the guinea pigs to make a cosy nest.

Your guinea pig should have a run (or another hutch) in the garden so that it can go outside in the summer. The run should be sturdy so that it cannot be accidentally knocked over. Always bring your guinea pig indoors at night.

saying hello

When your guinea pigs arrive, they may be feeling very scared. Place them gently in their hutch, and leave them alone for a little while so that they can get used to their new home.

Always approach your guinea pig from the front, not the side. Talk quietly to your pet – loud noises and shouting will frighten it.

▲ **Make sure your pets have fresh food to eat.**

Parent Points
Make sure your child knows how to handle the guinea pig before he or she tries to pick it up (see pages 16–17).

Handle with care

Make sure your guinea pig is used to you before you pick it up. Start by stroking it gently with one finger while it is eating, then use your hand. Don't pick up your guinea pig unless you are sitting or kneeling down. To pick it up, put one hand under its bottom and the other around its shoulders. Let your guinea pig sit in your cupped hands. If it starts to wriggle or squeal, gently put it back in its hutch. Never put the guinea pig on a table or chair, as it may fall off and hurt itself.

▶ **Speak gently to a timid guinea pig.**

▼ **Never squeeze or drop your pet.**

Looking after your guinea pigs

If your guinea pig has short hair, brush it once a week. If it has long hair, it will need brushing every day. Brush the fur in the same direction as it grows, and don't press hard.

▲ A guinea pig's teeth are growing all the time. Give your pet a block of wood to gnaw on. This will keep its teeth short and sharp.

▲ Make sure your guinea pig always has plenty of fresh water and food.

Parent Points
Take the guinea pig to the vet once a year for a check-up. If it is having trouble eating, or if it is drooling, its teeth may be too long and you should take it to the vet. A visit to the vet is also needed if it has persistent diarrhoea, runny eyes or a runny nose. Also check for flystrike every day especially during warm weather – check its bottom for fly eggs or maggots.

◄ **Brush your pet with a soft baby hairbrush. Put a towel on your lap to catch the hairs.**

Feeding your guinea pigs

Your guinea pigs should have two meals a day. Buy special guinea pig food from a pet shop. Make sure your guinea pigs always have clean food.

Guinea pig food

Kale

Chicory

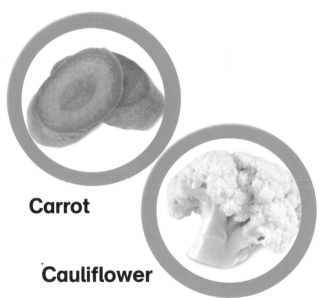

Apple

Your guinea pigs will enjoy being fed treats, such as a slice of apple and carrot sticks and other pieces of fresh fruit and vegetables. Always wash fresh foods before you feed them to your pets.

Carrot

Cauliflower

Parent Points
Make sure the guinea pig isn't given too much lettuce or cabbage. Vitamin C is important to keep your guinea pigs healthy – check with your vet. Never feed them raw greens or runner beans.

Keep it clean

Your guinea pigs' hutch needs to be kept clean. Once a day, use the scoop to clear out any droppings and dirty hay, and to remove any old bits of food. Put in some fresh hay. Wash the food bowls. Clean the water bottle with a special brush.

Once a month, give the hutch a really good clean. Throw away all the old newspaper, wood shavings and hay. Wipe the hutch down with disinfectant and water. When the hutch is dry, put in fresh newspaper, wood shavings and hay.

Always wash your hands after you have cleaned the hutch.

◀ **While you are cleaning the hutch, keep your guinea pig in a box, their exercise area or the outdoor run.**

▶ **Don't forget to clean your pet's bowls.**

▼ **Once a week change the bedding completely. Throw away the old bedding and put in new, clean bedding.**

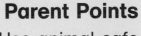

Parent Points

Use animal-safe disinfectant (available from pet shops) for cleaning the hutch.

Don't worry if you see the guinea pig eating its own droppings – this is natural, and it ensures that the animal is getting full nutritional benefit from its food.

Your guinea pig's life cycle

▼ At about five weeks a female guinea pig can have babies of her own.

③

①

◀ A newborn guinea pig has hair, and can see and walk.

②

▲ Guinea pigs suckle or drink their mother's milk until they are 3–4 weeks old.

Let's explore!

Guinea pigs do not play with toys, but they need lots of exercise and like to explore. You can make an exciting indoor guinea pig playground in an old drawer. Inside the drawer put some old cardboard boxes and open-ended plastic tubing. Cut holes in the boxes for your pets to crawl through. Or put the boxes and tubes on the floor so you can see the fun close up.

▼ **Young adult guinea pigs enjoy running through plastic tubes and exploring boxes.**

Saying goodbye

As your guinea pig grows older, it will spend more and more time sleeping. This is perfectly normal. Just make sure it is warm and cosy and feels safe.

If your pet is very old or ill, it may die. Try not to be too sad, but remember all the fun you had together. You may want to bury your pet in the garden.

▼ **When your pet is awake, stroke its fur gently. If it is breathing strangely, tell an adult at once.**

Squeaker last summ

My pet Squeaker

Remember all the fun you had together

Guinea pig checklist

Read this list, and think about all the points.

✔ Guinea pigs are not toys.

✔ Treat your guinea pig gently – as you would like to be treated yourself.

✔ How will you treat your guinea pig if it makes you angry?

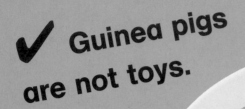

✔ Most guinea pigs live for about seven years – will you get bored with your pet?

✔ Animals feel pain, just as you do.

✔ Will you be happy to clean out your pet's hutch every day?

✔ Never hit your pet, shout at it, drop it or throw things at it.

Parents' checklist

● You, not your child, are responsible for the care of the guinea pig.

● It's best to keep at least two guinea pigs of the same sex together from the same litter.

● Can you afford a hutch for the house and a run for the garden, food, bedding and vet's bills?

● The hutch will need to be kept in a quiet place, away from draughts and direct sunshine.

● If you go on holiday, you will need a responsible person to feed, exercise and clean the guinea pig(s) or they will need to go to a holiday home.

● Guinea pigs are very timid. They are not suitable pets for a family with very young children, lots of children, or boisterous children.

● Exotic breeds of guinea pig are not suitable pets for children.

● If your child gets bored with cleaning out the hutch every day, it will become your job.

● Guinea pigs can get on well with rabbits if they are brought up together, but a cat or dog will frighten them.

● Always supervise pets and children.

Guinea pig words

The long hairs on a guinea pig's face are called **whiskers**.

A guinea pig has **claws** on its toes.

A guinea pig's fur is called its **coat**.

A group of guinea pigs which are all born together is called a **litter**.

Index

arrival of pet 14–15
babies 24–25
bedding 10, 23
brushing 8, 18
carrier 10
checklists 30–31
cleaning 22–23
coat 6, 32
company for pet 8, 9
death 28–29
droppings 22, 23
exploring 26

food 11, 15, 18, 20–21
food bowls 11
gnawing block 11, 18
handling pet 4, 15, 16–17
hearing 13
hutch 9, 10, 12–13, 31
cleaning 22–23
illness 19, 29
life cycle 24–25
life span 4, 30
litter 8, 32
long-haired pets 8

outdoor run 10, 13
play 26–27
rabbits 9, 31
short-haired pets 8, 9, 18
sunburn 27
teeth 18, 19
types of guinea pigs 6–7
vet 17, 19
water bottles 10, 22
whiskers 32